Dew Drops

Collected Poems

of

Denver Welte

Copyright

Denver Welte

Dew Drops
Denver Welte
Dew Drops © 2010-2016 Denver Welte

All rights reserved under International and Pan-American Copyright Conventions. All characters in this publication are entirely fictitious and any resemblance to real persons, living or dead, is purely coincidental.

First English Language edition 2016
Welte, Denver 1982
Cover Art by Bryan Costales

Softcover: ISBN 978-1-945232-06-0
Kindle: ISBN 978-1-945232-07-7
eBook: ISBN 978-1-945232-08-4
PDF: ISBN 978-1-945232-09-1
Audio Book: ISBN 978-1-945232-10-7
Hardcover: ISBN 978-1-945232-11-4
HTML: ISDN 978-1-945232-12-1

Published by

Fool Church Media
Published in the United States of America
http://www.foolchurch.com

Preface

This book was compiled from poems written over three years. Most were originally presented for free on www.bcx.news under the blog "Dew Drops."

The title of this book echoes that original blog name. Although that blog has been retired, all those poems and more have been collected into this book.

Denver Speaks

I wrote many of these poems when in the beginning stages of my recovery from alcohol. A recovery that was made possible because of my supportive, loving family. I wrote these poems to reflect rather than regret. I've grown and changed in many ways. I let go of my addictions and became a mother to my amazing son. My life is something I am now truly grateful for.

Denver Welte

DARKNESS

˜We can easily forgive a child who is afraid of the dark; the real tragedy of life is when men are afraid of the light.˜
— Plato

If You Knew Me

If you knew me you'd
probably know that I'm a sweetheart and it shows

If you knew me you'd
see a girly girl who likes to strike a pose

If you knew me you'd
show interest in everything I chose

Maybe if I knew you
I wouldn't want to smash your head in with a brick

Maybe if I knew you
something more civilized, like beat you with a stick

Maybe if I knew you
I'd understand you're just a pathetic prick

Here's a little gem for you
Making my tragedy front page news

Did you hear about the girl
who's life was almost lost in the sea?

Denver Welte

Did you hear about the girl
who lived in misery?

Would you have written about the girl lost at sea?

Called it a gem and put down your pen?

And felt good when you were done with the story?

If you knew me

Good-bye

Good-bye old friend, old enemy.
Remember me! Just one of many.

You were there when I was weak.
You took my hand, you held my cheek.

You told me I wouldn't feel a thing.

I trusted you.
I followed you.
I gave and gave and gave.

Until I was left on my heels with
Sand in my hands and rocks in my feet.

You thought you had the best of me.
You only had the end of one part of me.

Denver Welte

Bleed

Anticipation, irritation consume my every thought

Mini Miracles in play as the day trudges by

I sit with you on my knee as tears fill my eyes

I pinch myself until I bleed

My blood is sweet inside of me

Once bitter with poison dancing in my mind

Tainted soul, tainted life

I've surrendered yet still I bleed

Haunted

Sometimes I feel haunted and overstuffed.

In this strange body of mine I've had enough.

Life is a gift and I should be grateful.

I find myself more jaded and wasteful.

Hateful in my thoughts, consumed by my dreams.

Was being happy ever after meant for me?

Time will tell and I will see.

What this life has in store for me.

Denver Welte

Tortured

Tortured soul didn't have a chance.

Born with the pain, you couldn't
remember from the past
brought from the last.

Trying to retrieve those memories,
run them out before they take
you over and turn you out.

Transport the pain, implant the brain
Immortal soul, how many lives will you take?

How many till you finally break?

Fear

You keep me chained in a what-if wonderland.

Bouncing bad ideas off my head hoping one might stick.

Still with me when I sleep, nightmares so dark so deep.

I've forgotten what it feels like to just be me.

You keep me checking for what I missed.
Did he? Did she? So paranoid, so pissed.

I've kept you alive and strong for far too long.

You are Fear. You steal all that is logical and good.

I will not be robbed anymore.

Denver Welte

Far Away

Why can't you see
the curse you left on me?

A burden I'll bear for eternity.

The peace of mind
I'll strive to find.

Keeping you far away

For if you get too close,
it will be my loss, my ghost.

Lost

Lost inside myself

No way out but in

Undeniably passive, easily overlooked

Pondering what could have,
would have, should have been.

Wasting precious moments with sin.

Trying to fill that empty place within.

So dark, so buried,
can't see to find the candle I need.

Yet still I search

Denver Welte

Baby Voice

Since I was five they've wanted you gone

You weren't strong enough

Undeniably passive, easily overlooked

This baby voice really took

Was it the feminine quality I sought?

Or something else deep inside me?

To this day I use you without knowledge

So small, so sweet

So fragile, so bleak

Little baby voice inside me

Will you ever go away?

Or will you always be a part of me?

Told What To Do

No one likes advice or to be told what to do
The thing is this creates a resentment or two

Authority comes in many different forms
In one way or another we try to conform

Employers, government officials, police officers, it's true
The more obvious ones who like to tell you what to do

No one likes to be told what to do

So take a look in the mirror and ask yourself, do you?

Denver Welte

Checking

Caught up in the chaos of my mind,
wasting time.

What a gift it is to be young,
only concern, HAVE FUN!

Maybe, I'll relive this with my son.

Check this, check that!
gonna have a heart attack!

I wonder,
were they talking about me?

I know I shouldn't give a fuck,
and it's getting harder to breathe.

Wake up please and try to conceive,
positive thoughts that enter with ease.

I'm falling, falling to my knees.
Help me get up, help me to see.

Who Am I

Who am I if not a girl
without my hair so rare and red?

Who am I if not blue eyed?

Who am I if I don't cover my freckles
from side to side?

Who am I without the blues
purples & pinks placed so particularly
on my face on my cheeks?

What are my instincts?
It's been so long

Consumed by you took years away

So withdrawn

Who am I
but a girl

Denver Welte

Wrong For Trying

I saw you lying there on the cold concrete floor

I picked you up, hoping to give you more

Didn't know quite what to do.

I could see on your face, neither did you!

As soon as life returned to your eyes

I took you outside. I knew what to do.

My hopes were so high for you

I was wrong for trying to rescue you.

Damn Wind

Damn wind go away.

I can feel you on my face.

You leave my hair an absolute disgrace.

Damn wind please leave me alone.

I swear you exist to annoy me.

Damn wind. Cut you loose and you seek to destroy me.

Damn wind. More trouble than good it seems.

I challenged you once. You looked at me.

It wouldn't be long before I could see.

How strong a force you could truly be.

Denver Welte

The End

Deep breath caged-in unseen life barely heard
Take a deep breath, let it all in
Swim down the slopes of my twisted within
Mingle with the melody of cries never answered
Don't speak to the little girl when you pass her
She's full of promises and lies
Laugh at her when you get to the end
If you get to the end
Let it all out, don't scream too loud
It's only a dream
These things are not seen.

Dew Drops

Last Hurrah

A common release burdens us all
In with the good, out with a fall

Is this really it, the last hurrah?

So many years together we've spent

What have I gained? Pleasure or pain?
Nothing to show for the release I've obtained

You're just holding me back
Not helping, not letting me be

So I'm saying good-bye
It's kind of upsetting

I wish you the best
I regret all the spending

I'll last longer now
In this body of mine

Without your cloud surrounding me
I'll be just fine.

Denver Welte

Wake-Up

Why do I wake up this way?
Not yet ready to face the day?

Contemplating things ahead?
Can't I just go back to bed?

Do I really have to go out there?
Put on makeup, comb my hair?

Why can't I sleep a tranquil sea of undisturbed serenity?
Travel off to unknown lands like Peter Pan and Wendy?

Never get old and always live happily?

Why do I wake up this way?
Not yet ready to face the day?

Dew Drops

So Cold

So damn cold
A bathtub filled with ice
So cold

Barely melting
Just enough to break free from my skin

I don't notice
the white hairs attached
So cold

But it's getting warmer
the ice is melting, turning into water

I wonder why it's not sticking?
what's causing this change?
So cold

It was me all along
I wanted this pain
I made a decision
I'll make this one as well
I'll play by your rules

Guess it'll be warmer today

Denver Welte

Underneath

The power it once held
overwhelmed my memories

So strong it almost
took me

I almost let it
consume me

It confused me to the point of
insanity

I almost stand above it now
firm and strong

Unwilling to let it take
its hold on me

I'm moving on
but I'll never forget

What lies underneath
my surface

Step-In

A cloudy room filled with devastation.
Breathe in the condensation.
Fill your mind. Fill your head.
Who knew there was so much space.

Tiny pictures, all mixed up.
Place them in a plastic cup.
Drink'm down.
You'll get full.
Step into my cloudy room.

Denver Welte

Waiting

Waiting on what was
Waiting on what should have been

Waiting for months

Waiting for years

I hate waiting, it only brings me tears

Foggy

Feeling foggy
a little dazed
lots of music
a smoky haze
Strong and Thick
oh no here I go
feeling foggy
time to go

Denver Welte

Glance

Walked down the street
Knowing where you were going

Came across a place
Showing interest

Walked inside
Gave it a glance

Took a chance
All it took was a glance

Dew Drops

Snowed In

On a plane
A new beginning
out of the rain.
Fly, fly, fly away.
Escape to live another day.
Everything's fine
everything's great.
La, La, La-la
live to play.
Yet slowly drift away.
Didn't even realize
I was being buried alive
By an avalanche
built by a bottle a day.
La, La, La-la down I go.
I knew I didn't really
like the snow.

Denver Welte

LIGHT

˘There are darknesses in life and there are lights,
and you are one of the lights, the light of all lights.˘
—Bram Stoker, Dracula

Another Day

Another day passes.
I close my eyes

I start to think of all the things
I didn't do.

The list grows and flows
into the next day.

I remember walking down
that concrete LA street with you.

Just a girl, still a child.

I remember the heat reflecting
onto our faces.

And asking you Dad,
what would you have more of?

"Time or money?"
"Time," you said.

I agreed and we continued,
to walk that LA street.

Denver Welte

Edge

The last time I stood
on the edge of a cliff

I closed my eyes, stepped off
and didn't give a shit.

I didn't feel the ground before it ended.

I didn't know gravity would take me.

I felt permanently suspended.

It wasn't till I hit the bottom
and lost my voice

I realized that's it.
Time to make a choice.

Now I feel the earth beneath my feet.

I feel the wind on my face.

Now I feel there are cliffs all around me.

Now I feel.

The Way I Felt Then

The way I felt then
is the way that feels best.

I wore that way like a medal
proud and shiny and new.

The way I felt then
was so beautiful and true.

My dreams needed no thought
I just knew they'd come true.

The way I felt then
is how I want to feel now.

With patience, kindness and love
I will get there somehow.

Denver Welte

Headspace

I waited so long for ya,
tick tock.

Filled in my headspace
with what could go wrong.

Just goes to show,
you never know until ya do it.

Before ya know it,
the fear's consumed ya.

Before you had a chance
to be the real you.

So let it go,
breathe and just know.

Happiness can be obtained.

Bypass the brain
and look into your soul.

Tiny Pebbles

I closed my eyes and searched for silence

I felt tiny pebbles beneath my feet

I looked down at them and they started talking to me

They wondered why I searched
for something they could not see

Why I would take the time, make the time
for something so seemingly silly

I smiled in response as their wonder made me think

Well my tiny friends the answer isn't bleak

Simply said there's more to life
than tiny pebbles beneath my feet

Denver Welte

Today

Today I can see

I can hear

I can breathe
I can feel your arms wrapped around me

Today I can smell the scent of your skin so well

Today I can kiss you
Taste you
Love you

Today you are here
Today I can smile

Butterfly

A butterfly landed on my nose
I flinched and crinkled my toes

It opened its wings and gave me a show
Showed me things I didn't know

As it flew away I couldn't even blink
So beautiful I shook my head, I had to think

The future looks pretty sweet

Denver Welte

Dexter

Oh little dog Dex, with your floppy ears
and your wrinkly neck.

Such a mess you make,
so many pee-pee mistakes.

Well, we love you nevertheless.

Under the covers is where you'll rest.

Our little Dexter, our little love.

Your mother was a Basset,
your dad a Shar-Pei.

Now in between us you lay.

We will love you for now and always.

Little Socks

Soon life is going to change.

Sure my eye shadow and lip gloss might stay the same.

Crap! I still have to think of a name!

Oh little one on the way, the thought of you brings tears to my eyes.

Scares the s--- out of me at the same time.

Little Laska or other. Can't hardly wait to be your mother.

Find little socks that match each other.

Until we meet, I'll sit and dream
of putting little socks on those little feet.

Denver Welte

Mom

What a lady you are
My own personal super star.

They say, "No one loves you like a mother."

In fact it's true. I'd never want another.

Through it all, you've been there
like no one else could be.

You're so much more than a beautiful mother,
you're a wonderful person to me.

Today's your day.
We'll sing out Happy Birthday to thee.

I love you mom.
I always will, unconditionally.

Wake Up

Wake up and clear your mind.

Put on the coffee in your own time.

Wake up the worlds outside.

Put your hand in mine, lets explore this world together.

Once rejected like a break-up letter.

This time it's ours for the taking

When it's ours it's worth making right.

This time it's yours and mine.

Just wake up and step outside.

Denver Welte

Alone

Alone I am colorless and cold.

Alone I am a question without an answer.

Alone I am a sinking stone with no bottom.

Alone I am a shadow with no reflection.

Alone I am small and cannot grow.

Alone I am doubtful and afraid I'll never know.

Alone I am guarded and I don't want it to show.

Alone I am unable to see myself complete.

When I am with you I know I'm where I need to be.

Sister

Little sister standing outside of my plane.

Tears streaming down your face

Wondering when I'll see you again.

Little sister with your Mickey Mouse toys & simple joys.

Golden hair, tangled and knotted, only brush it if you dare.

Thirsty for milk and nothing else.

Purple hair one of the many colors you'll wear.

So smart, so sweet.

If we weren't sisters, we'd probably never meet.

Little sister you'll always be much more than a sister to me.

Denver Welte

Framed

Frame of mind

Framed my mind

Four corners, sealed inside

Sheet of glass hard to pass

Dust settles and turns to ash

Burn my past, flames surpass

Break the glass

I'm free at last

Frozen

Surprise. It's me.
I haven't fallen yet.

Caught by my own translucent little net.

Surprise. It's me.
And I don't carry that regret.

You say, "Don't assume, it's not in our teachings."

Then why are you simply believing
the shit you are thinking?

Surprise. I'm still standing.

Just wanted you to know,
Don't be surprised when I continue to grow.

Denver Welte

I Do

You say that you're true,
you love me and I'm sure you do.

Thanks for the trips, the hotels, the kisses
you left on my skin.

Only to leave and make me
Miss you again.

Thanks for the memories,
they were nice.

Now it's time I became your wife.

Annoyed night by night
By your snoring.

I wake up, look at you
And keep adoring.

I love you then, now,
And forever.

I can't wait to hold
Our baby together.

Dew Drops

Four Dogs

Four dogs today.
Four dogs all different, completely the same.

Short and small, legs barely two inches tall!
not very smart, with the biggest heart.

I love them all!

They'll never know how much they have,
and they'll never care.

So great in their simplicity,
Love and be loved by all.

Amazing what we can learn from them,
These creatures large and small.

Oh how I love them all.

Denver Welte

Human

Certain people seem to know their place in life.

Comfortable in human form.
Knew where they were going since they were born.

Some lose their way.
Take a wrong turn.
Just want to play.
Escape the pain they've hidden away.
Learn a lesson or two along the way.

Trying so hard to live by society's rules
Only to learn one day these are the biggest fools.

True happiness lies within the spirit of you.

New Life

I'll never forget watching all those movie
in the dark "Batman", "Spiderman"

Their adventures were nothing compared to
what we were about to embark.
You've brought people together

They've traveled hundreds of miles
to see your little face smile.

The joy you can spread just laying in your bed!
I'm impressed little one, the best is still to
come.

The sound of your laughter like
nothing else I've heard.

Angels couldn't sing a better melody
through the song of a bird.

My cheek's sore from smiling
my eyes low from crying.

My life starring "Westley"
Wouldn't trade it for the world.

Denver Welte

Melting

Soft kisses fall from your lips
and dance on my skin.

Penetrating the shield
I've built from within

Melting the hurt, the pain,
the tears that I've cried.

Letting you in
I now feel alive

Reflections

A blank face stares into
a reflection of a building.

But does not see a face
staring back.

Just the blinding sun
and what was once

A face, maybe a smile.
Maybe the happiness of a young child.

Buildings are being built every day.

Denver Welte

Old Into New

Starting over and still so young

A little strange, a little fun

The new me sits on an old stage

Waiting for the act to begin

The leading man still missing

What else is new?

I am, I am, does that count for much?

Surrounded by all this once new, now old stuff

Hope

Just yesterday or a million years ago.

It took seemingly endless amounts of tears
to fill my soul and float back to the surface.

It took so many broken dreams to think
that one could actually be fixed.

The tears come less often.

The doubts though still there
Come with less force.

The hope lies beneath my feet.

Denver Welte

Speak

They asked her to speak.
She felt like a freak.

Was she simply there to amuse them?

A side show at best.
Yet she couldn't contest.

She fed them her lines they said, "Thank you."

Are they blind? Can they hear her?

Why smile, can't see it.
Why speak, can't hear it.

But then something changed.

And to her surprise
She started to feel tears in her eyes.

She kept coming back and before long she knew

She was where she belonged
Simply stated, and true.

Memories

So many memories trapped in one place.

Slowly dissipate with each step I take.

Once just company, now I lay, I sleep
and wake up each and every day.

Time has passed, people have passed.
New people have come. Old memories
fade with each step that I take.

Denver Welte

Clouds

I watched the clouds move today.

It's been a long time since I've seen them dance that way.

I watched the clouds move today.

I'd forgotten how fast they can sway.

I took out the trash for the first time in months.

I'd forgotten how much it sucks.

Can't help but smile as I toss out the roses you bought me on the silly holiday.

What a waste, you'd say, still they made me happy for a moment that day.

Said good-bye again yesterday.

I wonder if you watched us drive away.

I watched the clouds dance today.

This Place

I never thought we'd be at this place.

A place where the decisions we make
Involve choosing green or blue paint.

A place where I could wake up next to you,
And not smell vodka on your face.

Oh wait that was me.

Your's was more happy, but light, that's right.

A place where our adventures start at Lowes,
And end in grocery store rows.

A place where we can feel real love.

This place brings tears to my eyes,
The kind I don't mind to cry.

This place I never thought we'd come to,
You and I.

Denver Welte

Never Be The Same

Since the first day we met,
never will I be the same

A mother, a child, a gift
and a smile

Never the same

A cry, a heartbeat, and
a name

Never the same

A breath, an embrace, my heart
you take

Never the same

More meaning, more light, more life
Never the same.

Dew Drops

My Son, My World

A year ago today
is when we found out you were on the way

Now I stand over you
and watch you lay

Asleep on our bed
with sweet dreams in your head

Every year that goes by
you'll be reminded by the love in my eyes

That you were the gift
the ultimate grand prize

I couldn't have asked
for a more perfect present

My son, my world
My love

Denver Welte

Wonder

Never have I wondered more
For what's to come, for what's in store.

Day dreaming of you has become a hobby
Wondering what you'll look like, what you'll be.

If you'll look like daddy? If you'll be like me?
If you'll have his eyes, or if they'll be blue or green?

So many wonders still left unseen,
It's okay, just more time to dream.

My life is about to change for the better,
I don't doubt it whatsoever.

Drift

Why do some people
capture our hearts from the very start?

While others drift along,
a note in a song, never to be heard again?

The family ties that bind a few of us,
grow stronger year by year.

Other knots, never tight,
loosen and fade into the atmosphere.

I won't let go of those I know
are in my heart forever.

Denver Welte

Another Trip

Another haul, another trip,
another dip in our relationship.

Another you, another me,
another, "Who knows how long it'll be?"

Another thousand, another five.

how many more thousands will it take
before out relationship is at stake.

More time apart than together.
Married? Maybe never.

Grateful I am. Impatient more than ever.
We're about to have a baby together.

Free

Too many situations running through my head.

The outcome's never close
to what I've dreamed of in my bed.

Oh my God. Turn it off.

Just let me be!

This mind of mine
is playing tricks on me.

I just want to be free
and what's holding me back is me!

Denver Welte

Ladybug

I saw a ladybug today.

The ladybug I saw was stuck on a door.

Like it was meant to be there,
and it had been there before.

The next day there was on my shoe.
Looking up at me as if it knew.

Many days of my childhood were spent
collecting you.

I smiled at the bug,
and wondered what to do.

So many memories of then and now.

The ladybug flew away.
Like it had never been there before
And it was just another day.

Good-bye Friend

For too long now
I've inhaled your sin.

Let you in on all of mine.

Every heartache
every bottle of wine.

More than a habit, a crutch,
never wanted to like you this much.

Now it's time to let you go.

Angry moments ahead,
I'm sure I'll show.

Completely worth it in the end,
for what I'll have to show.

Denver Welte

Walk Away

To watch you walk away from me
    Gets harder every time.

Now that our souls have had the chance
    To truly intertwine.

You gaze at me silently
    As I read your mind.

You say the words I knew you would
    I look at you and you smile.

To watch you walk away from me
    Will be the hardest this time.

Really

Did you really just ask me if I wanted to go
Back to the place I lost part of my soul.
A part I never wanted to lose.
A part that makes it harder to even trust you.

Alone in the darkest part of my head
Going insane, wishing I were dead.
Really, did you just ask if I wanted to go back
to where my greatest disasters
held center stage.

For the seemingly inevitable psychotic rage
that built up inside me.
Do I want to go back?
You must really not know me.

I'm terrified to go back to the place
you let me go.
Sunk in water, buried in snow.
I poured my poison and drank it, it's true.
But go back to the place where I let it take me
from you?

I don't think so, and really do you?

Denver Welte

What Can It Be?

Squishy, squashy, ooey, gooey
red and bluey

what can it be?

stretchy, strong, short and long

what can it be?

green, orange, pink, blue

I don't know do you?

chewy sweet and tart

I know! I know!

I love these with all my heart

* * *

if you enjoyed this book, please review it on various book web sites, and recommend it using your favorite social media.

About The Author

Denver Welte is an American poet living in Eugene, Oregon with her fiancé and son Westley. She enjoys the outdoors and playing with her son.

http://www.foolchurch.com/people/authors/denver_welte

www.ingramcontent.com/pod-product-compliance
Lightning Source LLC
Chambersburg PA
CBHW032050090426
42744CB00004B/157